DYNAMITE DINOSAURS

written by Sarah Albee
reviewed by Robert E. Budliger

Reader's Digest
Children's Books

Pleasantville, New York • Montréal, Québec • Bath, United Kingdom

Dinosaur Mysteries

Dinosaurs have been **extinct** for 65 million years. And everything we know about them comes from the study of their fossilized bones, footprints, and some smaller bits. Considering this, it's truly amazing that we know as much as we do about these remarkable animals. But it is not at all surprising that so many mysteries remain.

Were dinosaurs warm-blooded like modern birds or cold-blooded like modern reptiles? Why would it matter? Warm-blooded animals need more food, and they grow quickly. If a huge dinosaur, such as *Brachiosaurus*, were warm-blooded, it would have needed to eat tons of **vegetation** every day—and its young would have taken about ten years to grow to full size. If it were cold-blooded, it would have needed much less food, but its young might have taken 100 years to grow to adulthood!

Camouflage or Color?

We don't know what colors dinosaurs were, but we can take a guess by looking at animals today. *Edmontosaurus* (top) **migrated** across open plains, so it probably had a coloring that matched its surroundings. *Coelophysis* (bottom) was a tigerlike creature, so it may have had stripes that helped it hide from **predators**.

Pumping Blood

How did a huge, long-necked **sauropod** such as *Barosaurus* circulate blood throughout its enormous body? How was its heart able to pump blood up its 30-foot neck and into its brain? Some scientists estimate that its heart would have had to weigh over 1½ tons to manage that task. Other scientists think that it must have had more than one heart. Since soft tissues like hearts don't fossilize, it's doubtful that we will ever know.

What's That Word?

As you read, you will see words that are in **bold** type. Look for them in the glossary on page 22 to learn what they mean.

5

Biggest and Longest!

The biggest of all the dinosaurs were the plant-eating sauropods. Sauropods had thick feet and legs (think "elephant") and very long necks, which were balanced by their long tails.

Although the sauropods' skeletons were huge, they were light. Pockets of air in the neck bones of these dinosaurs made their necks extremely light and allowed the animals to hold their heads upright and move them around easily.

Because sauropods were so large and because they traveled in herds, many meat-eating dinosaurs simply stayed away from them.

Most meat-eating dinosaurs were not huge. The biggest meat-eater discovered so far is *Giganotosaurus*. This dinosaur had lightweight leg bones, which allowed it to chase—and catch—fast-moving **prey**.

Stretching Necks

Mamenchisaurus (near right), *Diplodocus* (center), and *Brachiosaurus* (far right) were among the biggest and heaviest animals that ever lived. And they all had incredibly long necks with relatively tiny heads on top. A modern giraffe's neck looks short in comparison!

Heavy Duty!

Brachiosaurus was one of the largest and heaviest sauropods. But compared to other sauropods, it had a relatively short tail, which kept it from being ranked among the longest. By some estimates *Brachiosaurus* weighed up to 50 tons—as much as 10 bull elephants. It swallowed huge stones (called **gastroliths**) on purpose. These stones ground up the vegetation inside the animal's gut and allowed for digestion.

Brainy Business

Most of the small dinosaurs were meat-eaters, and they seemed to have big brains for their size. They also had relatively long legs and arms. How did they manage to survive living side by side with their much bigger meat-eating and plant-eating cousins? Scientists believe they made their homes in thick undergrowth or around craggy, rocky places where larger animals couldn't fit.

One of the smallest meat-eaters was *Compsognathus,* which was about 3 feet long. It had a narrow, pointed head, a flexible neck, and a tail that was long for its body's size. It probably ate large insects, lizards, and small **mammals**—it may even have swallowed them whole.

On the other hand, *Stegosaurus* had the smallest brain relative to its size. It was 25 feet long and had a brain the size of a walnut!

A Head Case

Troodon (top) had the largest brain relative to the size of its body. This sharp-eyed, birdlike **theropod** was probably a deadly hunter. *Tyrannosaurus* (bottom) had one of the largest heads, but its brain was relatively small. A human brain takes up most of the head and allows us the ability for complex thought.

Dino Speedsters

For many of the smaller dinosaurs, the best defense against predators was to run away. The speedier ones were usually able to outrun predators.

But many large dinosaurs had speed on their side as well. The speediest meat-eaters had small bodies and long back legs.

The fastest group of dinosaurs was probably the **ornithomimids**. These were meat-eaters that probably fed on small mammals, insects, and lizards (the group may also have included plant-eaters), and they stood about as tall as a human, although some were even bigger!

The ornithomimids resembled modern ostriches and may have reached speeds as fast as 40 miles per hour, allowing them to outrun much larger predators.

In the Fast Lane

Ornithomimids ran faster than a human but not as fast as an ostrich.

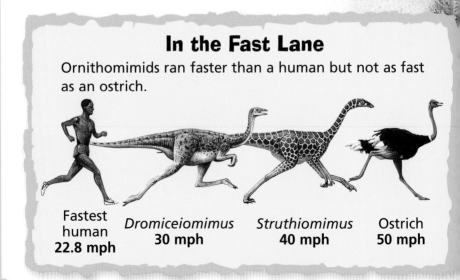

| Fastest human 22.8 mph | *Dromiceiomimus* 30 mph | *Struthiomimus* 40 mph | Ostrich 50 mph |

Gallimimus, the biggest
ornithomimid, ran so
quickly and changed
direction so suddenly
that it could easily
avoid the scary but slow-
moving *Albertosaurus.*

Good Defense!

Speed was no defense for slow-moving plant-eaters, but they had other ways of putting off predators. Size, for example. Some dinosaurs were so huge, no predator would even think of attacking them. Others defended themselves with horns, clublike tails, or skin as thick as armor.

Triceratops had bony frills and horns protecting its neck.

Boneheads!

A group of dinosaurs called **pachycephalosaurs** lived during the **Cretaceous** era. These dinosaurs had very thick skulls. Some had flat heads, while others had large, domed heads. Some scientists think these dinosaurs used their heads as battering rams, although new evidence indicates that the headgear may have been only ornamental—a show-off way to attract mates.

Tough Guys

The large meat-eating theropods were the terrors of their **Mesozoic** world.

Tyrannosaurus rex, which means "king of the tyrant lizards," was among the largest and fiercest of the dinosaurs. Its huge mouth held about 60 teeth, and each one was the size of a carving knife.

Before *Tyrannosaurus*, there was *Allosaurus*, which weighed almost 4 tons and was about the length of three cars. It stood as tall as an elephant. After *Tyrannosaurus*, there was *Giganotosaurus*. These three were among the biggest of the tough guys.

But plenty of smaller meat-eaters could be just as vicious, especially when they hunted in packs. *Velociraptor* and *Dromaeosaurus* were equipped with sharp teeth and deadly claws. *Ornitholestes* was probably no bigger than a human, but it weighed only as much as a medium-sized dog. Its prey included large insects, lizards, young dinosaurs, and small mammals. It may have grabbed its victims in its sharp claws and swallowed them alive!

Claws Count!

Utahraptor was less than half the size of *Tyrannosaurus*, but its fingers and toes had sharp claws. Each hind foot also had an extra-large claw with a razor-sharp tip that never touched the ground. These "meat hooks" were more than 12 inches long.

Sharing the Earth

While dinosaurs dominated the land during the Mesozoic era, other, smaller land creatures coexisted with them. Many of these creatures—including early mammals—spent much of their time trying not to get stepped on or eaten by the dinosaurs. Yet some of them managed to survive the **Cretaceous extinction**—and their descendants share the earth with us today!

Marine reptiles swam in the oceans. Although many of them looked like dinosaurs, they were only distantly related. Fast-swimming, dolphinlike **ichthyosaurs** and slower-moving **plesiosaurs** hunted other marine animals for food. Alongside them swam turtles, sea crocodiles, and fish.

What Was on Land?

Snakes, lizards, moths, bees, cockroaches, and rodentlike mammals all shared the earth with the dinosaurs.

What Was in the Water?

Ichthyosaurus was just one of the marine animals that trawled the seas in search of other animals to eat.

High in the Sky

Up in the Mesozoic sky flew many different kinds of creatures—flying and gliding reptiles and, somewhat later in the era, early birds. Although some may have looked like flying dinosaurs, the **pterosaurs** were only distant relatives.

Feathered dinosaurs most likely did not fly. Their feathers were probably used to keep their bodies warm. Some of the pterosaurs were as small as sparrows, while others were as big as a small airplane! How could such huge bodies stay airborne? Their bones were long, light, and hollow and probably held pockets of air to make them even lighter.

Some scientists believe that pterosaurs clomped around on all fours and thus could not move well on land. But they may have been able to climb trees by pronging the bark with the claws on their wings.

The largest pterosaurs most likely did not fly, but rather hitched rides on air currents and glided along on their enormous wings.

Birdosaur?

The theory that modern birds descended from certain theropod dinosaurs (and not from flying pterosaurs) has been gaining popularity. Pterosaurs may have looked birdlike, but they did not survive the Cretaceous extinction. Certain two-footed theropods, on the other hand, probably looked a lot more like weird birds than like giant lizards.

Baby Talk

Like all birds and most reptiles, dinosaurs laid eggs. At one time scientists believed that all dinosaur mothers laid their eggs and then went on their way, without staying around to care for their young—much the way modern turtles and lizards do. But recent discoveries have changed that thought.

While some dinosaur babies did not need help and were able to move about as soon as they were hatched, others depended on their parents for survival. Fossil discoveries show that some dinosaur parents built nests for their eggs and stayed nearby to feed and care for their young. But for how long? We just don't know.

Nursery Style

Dinosaur mothers laid their eggs in different ways. Some laid pairs of eggs in tidy lines. Others laid their eggs in an arc along the ground. Others lined the nest with leaves and plants to keep the eggs warm. Certain dinosaur mothers built their nests close together, probably for protection from predators.

Touchdown!

The biggest dinosaur egg discovered so far was about the size of a football. But considering how enormous some types of dinosaurs grew to be, dinosaur eggs were surprisingly small.

Glossary

cold-blooded: Having a body temperature that changes with the habitat; for example, snakes and lizards needing sun for heat

Cretaceous: A period of time that began about 145 million years ago and ended about 65 million years ago

Cretaceous extinction: The massive die-off of the dinosaurs at the end of the Cretaceous period

extinct: Gone forever

gastroliths: Fossils of stones that sauropods swallowed to aid digestion

ichthyosaurs: Marine reptiles with dolphinlike bodies that lived in the Triassic and Jurassic seas

mammals: Warm-blooded animals that have hair (at some stage of their life) and feed their young milk produced by the mother

Mesozoic: The Age of Dinosaurs era, which began about 245 million years ago and ended about 65 million years ago

migrated: Traveled regularly from one place to another, often from season to season, usually to breed or search for food

ornithomimids: A group of plant-eaters and meat-eaters that were the fastest of the dinosaurs; resembled the modern-day ostrich

pachycephalosaurs: A group of plant-eating dinosaurs with domed heads; referred to as the boneheads

plesiosaurs: Long-necked, slender marine reptiles ("near lizards") that thrived during the Jurassic and Cretaceous periods

predators: Animals that hunt other animals for food

prey: Animals that are hunted by other animals for food

pterosaurs: Flying reptiles that evolved during the Late Triassic period

sauropod: A plant-eating dinosaur with thick feet and legs, similar to those of the modern-day elephant

theropod: A meat-eating dinosaur, usually with small forelimbs

vegetation: Plant life

warm-blooded: Having a body temperature that stays the same when the temperature of the habitat changes